D0387586

CITY OF RANCHO MIRAGE

PUBLIC LIBRARY

Presented By:

**THE
ANNENBERG
FOUNDATION**

FORM 4(6/95)

STEFFI GRAF

TENNIS CHAMP

By Philip Brooks

Children's Press®
A Division of Grolier Publishing
New York   London   Hong Kong   Sydney
Danbury, Connecticut

Photo Credits

Cover, Focus on Sports; 5, ©Bob Martin/AllSport; 6, ©Mitchell B. Reibel/ Sports Photo Masters, Inc.; 8, ©Russell Cheyne/AllSport; 9, ©Gary M. Prior/AllSport; 10, Focus on Sports; 13, ©Bob Martin/AllSport; 14, Reuters/Bettmann; 16, 19, ©Gary M. Prior/AllSport; 20, ©Mike Powell/ AllSport; 22, Focus on Sports; 25, UPI/Bettmann; 27, Focus on Sports; 28, ©Simon Bruty/AllSport; 30, 33, Reuters/Bettmann; 35, AP/Wide World; 36, ©Matthew Stockman/AllSport; 38, ©Simon Bruty/AllSport; 39, ©Rob Tringali, Jr./SportsChrome East/West; 40, AP/Wide World; 43, ©Clive Mason/AllSport; 44 (left), ©Mike Powell/AllSport; 44 (right), ©Russell Cheyne/AllSport; 45 (left), ©Bob Martin/AllSport; 45 (right), ©Gary M. Prior/AllSport; 46, ©Rob Tringali, Jr./SportsChrome East/West; 47, ©Rob Tringali, Jr./SportsChrome East/West

Editorial Staff

Project Editor: Mark Friedman
Design: Herman Adler Design Group
Photo Editor: Jan Izzo

Library of Congress Cataloging-in-Publication Data

Brooks, Philip, 1963–
    Steffi Graf : tennis champ / by Philip Brooks.
      p. cm. – (Sports stars)
    Summary: A biography of the West German tennis player who won her first Grand Slam tournament at seventeen and beat Martina Navratilova to win her first Wimbledon tournament in 1989.
    ISBN 0-516-04397-8
    1. Graf, Steffi, 1969–   —Juvenile literature. 2. Tennis players— Germany—Biography—Juvenile literature. [1. Graf, Steffi, 1969– 2. Tennis players. 3. Women—Biography.] I. Title. II. Series.
GV994.G7B76   1996
796.342'092–dc20   95-40244
[B]   CIP
                                       AC

STEFFI GRAF

TENNIS CHAMP

Steffi Graf became a professional tennis player when she was just 13 years old. By the time she was 21, she was the most unbeatable athlete in any sport. No one could touch her. She was more unstoppable than Michael Jordan or Troy Aikman.

All the players on the women's pro tennis tour can hit the ball hard. All are strong and quick. Steffi Graf is stronger and quicker than any of her opponents. And she can hit a tennis ball harder than any of them.

Steffi remembers playing tennis when she was a child in the German village of Brühl. It was so easy. It seemed she was born to slam her high, powerful forehand. "I always wanted to hit [the ball] hard. It's just in you as a child. You pick up the racket and you just play." Steffi has always loved to play tennis.

Steffi (center) with her parents

When she was 13, Steffi began playing in tournaments for young players. She hoped to qualify for the professional tour. Her mother, Heidi, practiced and traveled with her. In those first few years, Steffi had little success against older, stronger players. But she learned what it took to be on the professional tour. "You travel," she says. "You learn how to lose, and you learn how to win."

As she grew, Steffi kept hitting the ball harder and harder. Even fellow professionals could not believe how powerfully she drove the ball. "It was scary out there," Helen Kelsi said after a match with Graf. Kelsi was one of the best players in the world at the time. She shook her head and sighed. "I was just trying to hit the ball back and I couldn't even do that!"

Steffi in action at the U.S. Open in 1989

★ ★ ★

Hitting a ball to Steffi's forehand (right-hand) side is a bad idea! Steffi glides smoothly to her right and reaches back. Swat! The force of her swing lifts her off the ground. The shot streaks across the net as if it is fired from a cannon. The crowd applauds. Steffi wipes her brow and strolls back to the baseline.

This is just another day at the office for Steffi. She is unbeatable and she knows it. But she never taunts her opponents by throwing her fist in the air or shouting. In tennis, players are expected to be polite. And Steffi is always polite.

In Germany, they call her *die Grafin*, the Countess. She is regal on the court, calm and cool. She behaves like a champion. If she disagrees with a call made by a referee, she does not argue or throw a tantrum. She just plays her game and overcomes the bad call.

Early in her career, Steffi was so good that her goal changed from winning matches to playing perfect matches. "I'm really playing myself out there," she said once. "The score is totally meaningless."

Steffi had a picture in her mind of her perfect match. She would win every point. Each serve would be her best. Every shot would be so well placed that her opponent could only miss. Of course, no one ever can be perfect. But Steffi believed she could be perfect. If she missed a shot, she believed she had failed.

Steffi gets frustrated with herself when she misses a shot, but she never lets her frustration show. If her powerful forehand is not quite right or if her serve is weak, she plays through it and wins, anyway. To win even when you are not at your best is the mark of a true champion.

Steffi usually practices at a tennis club near her home in Heidelberg, Germany. She chooses to play on the court farthest from the club building. There, Steffi is like a different person. She is not cool and calm. She smashes rackets, kicks over trash cans, and yells at herself. "I'm free then," she explains. "I can show my emotions. I can scream." Everyone needs to scream at times.

Tennis does not make Steffi want to scream. It's the world outside of tennis that makes her angry. Steffi likes being the center of attention when she's on the tennis court. But when she's off the court, she wishes some people would leave her alone.

Steffi dreams of being left alone, but she is very famous in Germany. She longs to blend in with the crowd, but photographers follow her everywhere she goes. Many male fans have even proposed marriage to her.

Steffi has countless fans around the world. In her home country of Germany, she is mobbed by fans wherever she goes.

Imagine what it would be like to have people watching every move you make. Whether you were in a good mood or bad, you'd have to smile and answer silly questions. People would snap your picture and ask you for your autograph. You couldn't go to the movies or a shopping mall without being swarmed by fans who want to touch you. That's what life is like for Steffi Graf.

It may be difficult, at first, to feel sympathy for Steffi. After all, she has chosen to play tennis professionally. The fans and media have made her rich and famous. But it is no wonder that she loves to leave Europe, at times, and travel to the United States. She enjoys walking around New York City, where most people do not recognize her. For Steffi, it is a welcome relief to go out for a stroll and be ignored.

Steffi remembers her early days in tennis as happy ones. Then, she and her mother practiced together in gymnasiums. Reporters, agents, and crazy fans did not bother her. No one paid any attention to her. She and her mother had fun playing cards while waiting in airports or in hotel lobbies. Maybe those days were the "perfection" she is searching for.

Most of Steffi's fans mean well, but some go too far. One of Steffi's worst nightmares came true in 1992. Monica Seles, another tennis star, was stabbed by a spectator during a match in Hamburg, Germany.

"Oh God," said Steffi when she heard the news. "I hope it's not one of my crazy fans." It was. The man said later that he intended to wound Seles in order to help Steffi.

Monica Seles (above) was attacked by one of Steffi's fans in 1992. Steffi was horrified when she heard the news.

The terrible attack of Monica Seles still haunts Steffi. Seles could not play for three years. During that time, Steffi regained her number one ranking, which she had lost to Monica. But she wishes she could have proven she was still the best by playing Seles and beating her. No one wants to win because an opponent cannot play. Seles was Steffi's toughest opponent. Steffi missed competing with Monica.

Steffi in a championship moment

To win a women's tennis match you must win two sets of games out of three (to win a set you must win six games). Steffi wins most of her matches in straight sets — meaning that her opponent never wins a set in the match. Many of Steffi's matches are over in less than an hour. Between 1987 and 1989, Steffi lost only six matches. In 1989, she won 31 in a row.

During this long winning streak, it was not fun to play against Steffi Graf. "She doesn't like to lose a single point," said Terry Phelps, an excellent tennis player who could offer no challenge to Steffi. "She's always like that, so intense. You'd think after a while she'd get bored."

Graf was the number-one player in the world by such a wide margin it really was almost boring. Longtime tennis great Chris Evert joked in 1988: "The players [on the women's professional tour] all wish she'd fall in love, get married, and have a baby!" Evert went on to tell what makes Steffi so great: "With me, the mental part of the game was always stronger than the physical. Martina [Navratilova] was always known for the physical aspects of her game. Steffi has both!"

Chris Evert was a leading tennis star while Steffi was establishing herself. Evert credits Steffi with being a terrific all-around player.

Today, the physical part of Steffi's game is giving her trouble. Her own body challenges her. She has suffered from all sorts of injuries. She's had a broken foot, sinus trouble that needed surgery, an aching wrist, and a bone spur in her back.

The pain limits her power and quickness. Winning is more of a challenge now. Gone are the days when she could simply blow away her opponent. Now she uses her mind as much as her powerful forehand. She must play smart and preserve her energy.

Steffi is hard on herself, perhaps too hard. But this relentless drive to greatness makes her nearly unbeatable. And she still loves the game. She's always loved it.

The Wimbledon tennis club in London, England

The most important word in tennis is "Wimbledon." Wimbledon is a tennis club in England. Every summer, the most prestigious tennis tournament of the year is held there. A player is not considered best in the world until he or she has won Wimbledon.

———————— ★ ★ ★ ————————

The atmosphere at Wimbledon is formal compared to the U.S. Open or other American tournaments. Many Americans travel to England to witness the event. Spectators wear their best clothes and snack on strawberries and cream. The Queen of England and various princes and princesses watch from the "royal box."

At Wimbledon, players are expected to wear white outfits and to behave properly. Steffi, who wears white by choice and keeps her long hair tied back, is a favorite of Wimbledon fans. Steffi finds Wimbledon challenging because the matches are played on grass courts. Most players are more familiar with the clay surface used in most other tennis clubs. On clay courts, the ball moves more slowly and bounces higher than on grass. This gives players more time to take a big swing to slam the ball. On Wimbledon's grass courts, players must rely more on their quickness to return fast-moving shots.

Martina Navratilova was the reigning champion at Wimbledon until Steffi defeated her in 1988.

In 1987, Steffi reached the finals at
Wimbledon for the first time. There, she was
defeated by six-time Wimbledon champ, Martina
Navratilova. Steffi felt almost honored to lose to
her idol. She could not imagine what it would
feel like to defeat Navratilova.

A year later, she received another chance.
In 1988, Steffi and Martina met again in the
Wimbledon finals. In the rematch, Martina
jumped out to a quick lead. She won the first
set and went ahead 2-0 in the second. She
appeared to be headed for yet another title.

Then, something happened. Steffi slammed
forehand after forehand for winners. When
Navratilova charged the net, Graf sent perfect
shots down the lines, just out of Navratilova's
reach. Soon, she tied the match.

Though she did not show it, Steffi was excited. She began to believe her time had come. She believed she could beat the best. Steffi felt very calm and strong. The center court at Wimbledon seemed to belong to her.

Steffi won 12 of the next 13 games. She came from behind to win the match, 5-7, 6-2, 6-1. Steffi said later, "I lost to Martina in the previous year's final in straight sets, but I went away from it thinking that maybe I could be good on grass at some point in the future. And the way Martina was playing...I didn't want to put pressure on myself to win. So the 1988 final was not so much a surprise but a kind of verification."

Steffi and men's champion Boris Becker hold their Wimbledon trophies.

Defeating Martina Navratilova was all the sweeter because Navratilova was Steffi's idol. The win marked a big change in women's tennis. Navratilova and Chris Evert were finishing their brilliant careers, and Steffi became the best in the world.

The 1988 Wimbledon championship proved that Steffi's hard work had paid off. "For some years, I had some fear at Wimbledon," she says. "I wasn't confident...and I wasn't sure that I had the right game or athletic abilities to do well there." She won again in 1989. She also won in 1991, 1992, and 1993.

Steffi played in the 1988 Olympics and won the women's tennis gold medal.

In 1995, Steffi was trying to win her sixth Wimbledon title. She had to take pain-killing shots before her matches because of the bone spur in her back. Then she had wrist problems that forced her to withdraw from the doubles competition. She was upset about this. Her doubles partner was to have been Navratilova. Martina had come out of retirement to team up with Steffi. It was not to be.

Earlier in the year, Steffi had endured a pulled calf muscle. Then, a severe case of flu forced her to withdraw from a tournament in Germany. She won the French Open, however, to regain her number one ranking just weeks before Wimbledon.

Injuries have challenged Steffi in recent years.

Tired and not feeling her best, Steffi still made it to the Wimbledon finals. She faced the number-two woman player in the world, Arantxa Sanchez Vicario. Steffi had just defeated Vicario in the French Open. Here was the rematch. It turned into one of the greatest contests in Wimbledon history. The two were very evenly matched. Vicario's specialty is returning shot after shot until her opponent makes an error. She did just that, playing brilliantly.

It was a hard-fought match, but in the end,
Steffi endured back and wrist pain to win. She
cried with joy. This had been her most difficult
challenge. It confirmed yet again that she ranks
with Navratilova, Evert, and Billie Jean King
as one of the greatest players ever.

Despite her injuries, Steffi returned to the top in 1995.

Steffi talks to one of her youngest fans.

Steffi is a difficult person to get to know. Even her friends are not sure sometimes what she's thinking. She likes people who are funny. "I need humor," Steffi says. "And I need other people for their energy—or I would spend too much time alone."

No one is sure what is in Steffi's future. If injuries continue to bother her, she may retire. Or, she might retire simply to escape the media. In 1990, the Graf family was nearly torn apart by news stories concerning their personal lives. Then, while trying to escape the photographers at a ski resort, Steffi slipped and broke her right hand. "Obviously, a year like that takes its toll on you," she said. "You try to know for yourself what the real problems are, what is right and wrong for you...and you change your mind so many times you make yourself crazy."

After her terrible year, Steffi became more independent. She distanced herself from her father, Peter Graf. Until then, she had done whatever he told her to do. He was her coach and mentor. In 1995, he was arrested by the German government and charged with cheating on taxes concerning Steffi's income. The scandal threatened to destroy Steffi's career.

Steffi fought back—on the court. Despite the distractions, she still wins almost every tournament she enters. Steffi Graf lives one of the most difficult lives of any modern athlete. Yet when she competes, she continually proves herself to be one of the best modern athletes.

C ★ H ★ R ★ O ★ N

1969 • June 14: Steffi Graf is born in Mannheim, West Germany.

1982 • Steffi wins West Germany's 18-and-under tennis championship. At age 13, she is the youngest champion ever.

1986 • At age 16, Steffi notches her first professional tournament win, defeating Chris Evert in the Family Circle Cup.

1987 • Steffi wins the French Open, her first Grand Slam singles championship.

1988 • Steffi becomes the third woman ever to achieve a Grand Slam by winning the Australian Open, French Open, U.S. Open, and Wimbledon all in the same year. She also wins the gold medal in women's tennis at the Summer Olympics.

1990	• Steffi misses more than two months of play due to a hand injury.
1992	• Steffi wins Wimbledon again, but she loses her number-one world ranking to Monica Seles.
1993	• Monica Seles is attacked by a fan who wants Steffi to be ranked number one again.
1995	• Steffi wins Wimbledon again after two years. After Monica Seles returns to tennis, Steffi defeats her in a dramatic U.S. Open championship. It is the eighteenth Grand Slam title of Steffi's career.

STEFFI GRAF

★ GRAND SLAM CHAMPIONSHIPS ★

Australian Open	French Open
1988	1987
1989	1988
1990	1993
1994	1995

U.S. Open	Wimbledon
1988	1988
1989	1989
1993	1991
1995	1992
	1993
	1995

★ ★ ★

About the Author

Philip Brooks grew up near Chicago and now lives in Columbus, Ohio, with his wife, Balinda Craig-Quijada. He attended the University of Iowa Writers' Workshop, where he received an M.F.A. in fiction writing. His stories have appeared in a number of literary magazines, and he has written several books for children. He is the author of *Games People Play: Japan* and *Michael Jordan: Beyond Air* (Children's Press), and *Georgia O'Keefe* and *Mary Cassatt* (Franklin Watts).